In the Key of Life

An Activational Journey to the Soul

Joan Cerio

Life Lines
Sedona, AZ

In the Key of Life
An Activational Journey to the Soul

First Printing 2007

ISBN 978-0-9786976-0-0

Library of Congress Control Number: 2007903172

Cover design: Jason Boles
Cover photograph overlay of Eye of God nebula courtesy of NASA.
Egyptian hieroglyphic photo courtesy of Jason Boles.

Interior Design: Rudy Ramos Design Studio
Interior Drawings: Joan Cerio

Life Lines
P. O. Box 47
Sedona, AZ 86339

Printed in the United States of America

To all who have touched my life in so many ways

and have always believed in me...

Now believe in yourselves.

And so it is.

Ho!

Contents

Introduction

Thank your for paying attention to your inner voice or inner feelings when you decided to read this book. This means that the writings and drawings you are about to discover will help you change your thoughts and empower your life.

Your higher self has guided you to this book. Trust there is a reason why you are drawn to read it. When you first read the book, you may not understand all of the writings. The meaning of the words will come into your awareness during the day to day unfolding of your life.

Through the connection with my higher self, and guidance from Archangel Michael, Archangel Metatron and Ascended Master Melchizedek, in separate automatic writing sessions, the writings and keys you are about to read were inspired. I then merely placed onto paper the words that entered my mind. Most of the writings were composed on different days. Originally I had no intention of compiling them into a book. It wasn't until months later, when I was typing them into the computer, that I realized the power and purpose behind them.

I later decided to add drawings in the form of sacred geometry. Sacred geometry is the blueprint of the cosmos, which describes the patterns of all creation and represents all consciousness everywhere. It reminds us of our essential core and connection to the oneness, without the filters of our life experiences. The drawings are the geometric representation of the energy of the writings and are taken in by the subconscious mind.

The subconscious mind has the ability to receive information in the form of symbols and record thousands of times more information than the conscious mind. Acting as a tape recorder of information, the subconscious mind does not judge what it receives, since its job is to simply play or record. It responds to repetition and feelings. So the more you read the book, look at and meditate on the drawings, and feel empowered by the words, the more likely you are to record these experiences in your subconscious mind.

One of the keys to recording over old tapes or patterns that no longer serve you is to consciously choose to change your beliefs and your behavior. The writings serve to activate your conscious mind. They provide new patterns into which new beliefs and behaviors can emerge. More importantly, as you incorporate different beliefs, you are changing your DNA, the blueprint of life. We are not destined to relive the lives of our parents and ancestors as once thought. It is through interacting with our environment that we affect our biology. Bruce Lipton, Ph.D. purports in his book, *The Biology of Belief, unleashing the power of consciousness, matter and miracles*, that thoughts and beliefs do have the power to change DNA.

While DNA is important to the continued functioning of the organism and the continuation of the species, it is also similar to the subconscious mind in that it is a recorder of information. It is vitally important to the evolution of a species that information is passed down to offspring. Otherwise, each subsequent generation would have to recreate the myriad of experiences that are normally cataloged in the DNA of our cells. For example, instinctual behaviors would have to be relearned, such as the suckling behavior of mammals.

Quantum physicists are now discovering we are moving from a third dimensional awareness to a fourth and fifth dimensional awareness. The download of higher consciousness information is needed to prepare us for the new energies and experiences that exist in a multi-dimensional universe.

For ease of discussion, the keys have been numbered and titled writings and drawings organized under a key. This organization may be familiar to your current perception, which implies that the universe is organized in a linear fashion. As you will read, the universe is not linear. You probably heard the expression "coming full circle." Creation spirals and forms interconnected circles. Perhaps you have felt that you completed a portion or cycle of your life only to find yourself in another similar situation. Although it may look similar, you are on another level of the spiral.

The image used on each key or chapter page is the image of the Flower of Life, which is the key to creation. It is comprised of a series of nineteen interconnected circles of the same radius, enclosed within a larger circle. All of the platonic solids (cube, tetrahedron, octahedron, icosahedron, and dodecahedron) that are the building blocks of creation are contained within the Flower of Life.

You will find that the journey to awakening continues like the spirals of life. Each time you finish reading all the writings, you complete one turn of the wheel of opening your mind to new thought patterns and higher levels of consciousness. After the last writing, reread the first one.

These subsequent readings will allow another level of your unfolding to occur. The thought patterns you are producing as you continue to reread the book form the Flower of Life.

The shaded image inside the Flower of Life on each key page is the Egyptian ankh. To the Ancient Egyptians, the ankh was the key to eternal life and embodied the principle of neutrality, the joining of masculine and feminine energies within each of us.

In the Key of Life facilitates opening your mind, instilling your power of thought, opening your heart to yourself, and awakening you to your divine essence, the truth of who you are. And so it is.

Forethoughts

Opening to oneness is about opening your heart to your true self. It's about falling in love with you. It is the experience of love made manifest in the most intimate way possible.

Life is all about unfolding. We start in a curled ball, warm and safe, contained in the bubble of the womb. Eventually we are forced through the birth canal causing more constriction. We arrive here on earth saying to ourselves, "Why am I confined in this body?" Soon we attempt to break free and test the limits of our power only to hear, "Don't do this, don't do that!" No wonder this time of life is named the terrible two's!

The emotional body requires unfolding as well. As we grow, our emotional self grows and emotional scars experienced in childhood run deep. One way to unfold the emotional body is through bodywork.

As an instructor in massage school, I co-taught a class called "Unfolding." The class was taught on the first day of school as a way of introducing some fundamental principles of bodywork. The students paired up, and one student laid on the floor in a somewhat contorted, contracted fashion. The other student's job was to unfold the first by observing and then moving her partner in small steps until she was lying on her back. The macroscopic act of unfolding each other mirrored the microscopic act of unfolding the body's tissues during massage. It is based on the premise that we come into this world contracted and the goal is to unfold.

I have been working on my own unfolding for years, and at the age of forty-five, I knew it was time to begin unfolding the core of my being. Within this core lies buried the truth of who I am, and I fervently wanted to know myself.

For years I wanted to visit Sedona, although I didn't know why at the time. After spending five days there in May of 2004, I knew I had to return. My life was in transition, and although it felt scary, I chose to make some more major changes. A year earlier, I had not only ended a fourteen year committed relationship, but also had helped my dog cross over. In the fall of 2004, I resigned from my teaching work at the massage school, left my family and friends, and moved to Sedona. I packed my car and drove across country, following some friends who were driving to Phoenix. I had no job lined up, just a potential room to rent. My intention was to start my life over, drink in the healing energy of Sedona, and concentrate on healing myself.

After a little over a month in Sedona, my pilgrimage was well on its way. I started to write as a way of purging myself of emotions and also to bring forth the words I knew had been waiting to be placed on paper. After receiving some sound and light code healing to open my heart and my throat chakras, I began to allow the words from my higher self to flow. As my pen brought each word into physical form, I noticed my first writing was about the apple on which I was snacking.

The apple has one purpose: to be the perfect apple so it will be eaten, releasing its seeds to be scattered about Mother Earth. How can I be more of me so that I can release the seen for the unseen? My seeds are hidden deep in my flesh. Only through my seeming demise do I pass on my life force. Think of the potential that sits in my bosom! I am the creator of a hundred "apple trees" or more! My true power lies under the flesh in my core. The apple knows it must surrender itself to release its power.

Similar to the apple, there comes a moment in a caterpillar's life that requires the ultimate act of surrender and faith. It knows it must allow for the death of one body in order to step into another that will allow it to reach the sky. Just like the caterpillar, deep within each of us is a butterfly waiting to fly.

I have experienced many levels of surrendering in my life. I think we experience dark nights of the soul to facilitate the process of surrendering. You probably have experienced at least one dark night of the soul. They are times in your life when you "hit a wall" and nothing seems to be working. It is obvious you need to change direction, although the new direction may not be clear. Circumstances may take you to a point where you have no choice but to surrender. Prior to leaving for Sedona, I had experienced perhaps my darkest night of the soul.

"Into the dark with you! Only there can you see what you are made of. Keep going. You haven't plunged deep enough yet. Let your mind stay out of it. This is gut work. When all glimpses of remembering even the faintest glow of light have vanished from your mind, you are ready to begin.

Now take a deep breath. Can't do it? Does the breath get stuck? Where? Why? You know the breath is the bringer of the life force. Has yours left you so soon? When all the life force leaves the body, so does the soul. Welcome to your dark night of the soul.

Do you want to live or die? Answer me! There is no maybe here, only yes or no, and be emphatic about it! It's really not a hard choice, just an either-or. One negates the other. Choose life you say? Then live it, not survive it. Thrive in it and enjoy it. Choose death? Can you totally and emphatically deny everything you've done, your vision for humanity, your power, and choose to leave the work you came here to do, you agreed to do, for the generations to come? How can you deny yourself?"

It starts with doubt. Who am I? Why am I? I don't have any special gifts. What can I do that has not already been done? I am restless. There is more, but I can't grasp it. My passion squirms inside my chest, longing to be freed. It calls to me daily, "What about me?" I still can't find it. It's too dark. I am not strong enough, not wise enough, and not clairvoyant enough to see it there. Yes, already in my heart. It pulls in on the chambers of my heart. "You shall not beat with the force of a king's army. You shall beat with the strength of a coward whose only power is used to hold herself back." The greatest fear is the truth that rests in my bones. I am more than dust, to which, I was told, I would return. I am the light of heaven on earth. If I die, perhaps I will forever forget my true self. I can skip through the pain, and come out on the other side refreshed and say, "Phew, that was a close call!" Now the test comes. When the journey to the center of my being has reached its destination, the acting out of my demise begins.

After going from job to job, profession to profession since I was sixteen, at forty-four I was convinced I would never find where I belonged. I would never find my passion. Maybe I don't belong here on earth. It doesn't feel like I even come from here. Why not go back? Just give up the search and go home.

I was literally be-side myself. I had left my body and watched it in slow motion moving closer toward the busy street. "Just one more step," I said to myself, "and I can end all of this pain." I looked up at the oncoming car. In that same moment, I returned to my body. I turned and stepped back, away from the road. I could no longer hold back the years of tears that had been held inside after each supposed failure. I cried from my gut until it hurt. I had reached the pit of my fear. It was vile, ugly and raw, and I knew in that same moment, my healing had just begun.

As the days went by, I felt the energy of Sedona clearing me of patterns that no longer served me. Old emotional trauma, that had never been released and had harbored itself in my body, surfaced in my mind. A memory, a smell, a song would come from the depths of my being and remind me of the pain I had cataloged in my cells. Tears started unexpectedly and flowed for what seemed to be hours at a time. I felt myself being transformed on a daily basis, and I decided to honor this transformation through ceremony. I called it my death and rebirth ceremony, for, just like the apple and the butterfly, I was letting go of the seen, my former self, to allow the unseen part of myself to surface.

I decided to conduct my death ceremony at dusk. Dusk is a magical time that symbolizes the day coming to completion, when the veils between heaven and earth are the thinnest, and so it felt appropriate to celebrate the completion of my former life at dusk. After listing all of my beliefs, attitudes and emotional patterns that no longer served me, I made a prayer stick from a small branch I found during one of my many walks. Using a pocketknife, I cut three symbols into the wood. The first was a deep hole. I used a black pen and filled in the hole with its ink. The hole symbolized the rut I felt I had gotten into in my life. I had become complacent and tried to convince myself that a well-paying career, a home and a family were my dream, similar to the dream of most Americans. The black symbolized the darkness in which I was immersed.

Next, I carved a long gouge in the prayer stick to symbolize the scars I had collected from the many deep wounds I felt in my life. I had amassed quite a collection, from abandonment to heart break to guilt to fear. These were just a few of the emotions I chose to transmute during my death ceremony.

Lastly, I carved the letter "D" into the stick. It stood for denial. Denial of so many things in my life had created a wall to my true self. It was my last bastion against my greatest fear and biggest denial. I had denied myself joy, self-love, and most of all, the truth of who I am.

I held the ceremony of the death of my former life two days before the anniversary of my father's passing, since on the anniversary of his passing, I chose to celebrate my rebirth. Just prior to dusk, I made a foil cup and took the paper on which I had written all my former beliefs, attitudes and old patterns that no longer served me, and tore it into pieces small enough to fit into the foil cup. I stated my intentions as I ripped it up and then struck a match. With gratitude and love, I chose to transmute all that the paper represented, and from the ashes arose the core of my being, my power and my divinity.

The next part of the ceremony was held at my favorite hiking place. As I walked along the path, I chanted the sounds that surfaced from my forgotten self. I turned my attention to the prayer stick I created. I spoke out loud the meaning of the carvings and my intention to bless them, thank them for the exceptional job they did protecting me during my own forgetfulness — and let them go. As I threw the stick as far as I could and watched it fly off into the arroyo, I yelled as if I wanted the whole world to hear me. "As I release this stick back to the earth, I release the past that it represents." Exhilarated, I continued to walk briskly along the path until I reached the place on the rocks next to the stream, where I chose to sit. Sitting near the water, I cupped my hands in the creek and brought them slowly over my head. "Let this water cleanse me of all of the beliefs and attitudes that no longer serve me and all of the emotional pain I carried for too long." Then I buried the ashes of the paper I had burned and sat and meditated in the evening light. I let the flow of the water take all of my thoughts with it. I chose to be wiped clean, purified of the old.

After I finished my meditation, I slowly began my hike back. As I started back, I noticed how differently I felt. I felt I opened my core and it was raw and pulsing. I smelled metal, ozone after a lightening storm, and sulfur from a lighted match all at the same time. Did I release too much too soon, I wondered?

At dawn on the morning of the anniversary of my father's passing, I held my rebirth ceremony. The night before, I had written a list of affirmations I chose to bring into my new life. I read these aloud in the morning light while facing Thunder Mountain. Taking the prayer stick I had made to symbolize my rebirth, I wired a seed and several small feathers to the stick to impart the energy of new life and new heights I knew I would attain. Holding it up to the sky I said, "I fill this stick with the energy of my intentions. As I carry this stick through life, I carry all that it represents as a reminder of my true self." I sang happy birthday to myself and smiled on the way home. Later, I found that awakening to my core or unseen self was energizing and draining at the same time. I went home and began to write.

Today I feel alone. I traveled to the depths of my being and found my vulnerability. Beginning the next chapter of my life is risky. Endings are sometimes difficult, and the difficulty comes as no surprise. What is surprising is the pain of rebirth. It is like going through the birth canal all over again, only this time I am the canal as well. There is no other safe place, nowhere to hide. It's me with me. The veils of what once was are stripped away. The armor that I placed upon myself years ago, lifetimes ago, is gone in an instant. Suddenly, I am left totally naked, totally free from anything that weighed me down. My shell has cracked wide open, and it feels like the eyes of the world are upon me. I never felt so vulnerable, so totally open. I asked for freedom, and now that it is here, I find myself without a clear focus, and my energy scattered. I would call myself back, but I don't know whom I am *calling. I know I do not choose to call back the person I was. Is this what it feels like to be God? To know that I am like an etch-a-sketch wiped clean and waiting for the next creation to appear is daunting. I am the sea of pure potentiality. I felt it in my body, so much power. I want to run away, and yet I know I must step into my power. It takes incredible courage to walk into it and say, "I am God incarnate. I am the divine in form. Now I create." Now I manifest, not from old unconscious thought patterns, but from each breath of my being and each word I utter. My entire being, in concert and harmony can, by virtue of its God Self, create by just being. There is nothing that needs to be done but be the outcome I desire. I desire peace. I desire the awakening of the people of this earth to their God Self. Now all that is left is to **be** the peace, **be** the awakening. Is manifesting really that easy? Maybe it only seems to be easy since I really haven't tried it yet, consciously. It's time to try, no not try, **be** it! I am peace. I am awakened. I am God incarnate. Breathe, Breathe.*

As I continue my journey of unfolding, I share my experiences with you to remind you that unfolding is a process. As you take in the thoughts and energy of this book, your life will also unfold. Thoughts are energy and they change matter. Once you unfold into your beautiful lotus you can "re-member" the forgotten pieces of your true nature. In unfolding to your true self, it is necessary to surrender to your higher self and trust that the path your higher self chose long before embodying in this lifetime is the perfect path for you here and now. This is what it means to be in the flow of your creation, and the more you are open to be in your flow and notice what is happening around you, the easier the unfolding.

Sometimes it is obvious we are going with the flow of our creation. In 1996, the federal government, my employer at the time, was downsizing. I was in the safety and health field, and I knew that if many of us were laid off, there would be fewer similar jobs in the private sector. So, I decided to change my career. Since I had worked mostly in the health and healing professions, I chose to stay in that field. Only this time, I chose to do something a little different. I chose the alternative health field.

My partner at the time had just completed massage school and had become employed there. I knew the owners of the school who, along with my partner, encouraged me to attend. I had never thought about becoming a massage therapist, and I didn't even know if I would enjoy the work. To sweeten the deal, the owners allowed a reduced tuition, which my partner offered to pay. At my current job, I knew I could easily be granted leave without pay status since there were severe budget issues in the agency at the time. As I had enough in savings to cover my expenses for six months, I decided to go with the flow.

Massage school opened me to my true self; so much so, I didn't want to go back to my government job. It was my fear around money and my sense of obligation that made me return. When I returned, I noticed how much I had changed. I no longer looked at "problems" the way I did before. My relationships with co-workers changed for the better. While the job was still stressful, I found an inner strength from which to draw.

It was difficult for me to leave a well-paying career. It took two years after returning from massage school to finally leave. Once again, the universe showed me the flow. Once I began making plans to resign, things started to fall into place like they did before I left to go to massage school. I discovered the payroll department had made a mistake in the date of my within grade salary increase and owed me thousands of dollars! Then I received a notice in the mail that I had overpaid my income taxes. How many times does that happen? My tax preparer had transposed some numbers, and I was owed a thousand dollars more! I used this as my seed money to start my healing practice.

Say "yes" to the call of your heart by taking the first important step toward your heart's desire, and the universe will guide you the rest of your way. Your security is directly proportional to your faith.

In my work as a healer, my clients occasionally experienced a healing crisis after a session where the symptoms got worse before they got better. It seems to be a law of nature that the pendulum must swing way to the other direction before it can come back into balance. Be gentle with yourself as you go through the labor pains of your rebirth.

It is my intention that these words and drawings help you on your journey of unfolding your true self, expand your consciousness, open your heart, accept the assignment you chose long before embodying, and bring the unique light of who you are to the world. As we all step forward into the light of that which we are, the pathway of our transition into the next dimensions becomes clear.

Key 1

*The dew on a leaf is but
the gentle tears of a bird
that left in grateful flight.*

▲ PURPOSE ▲

Stepping into your life's work is similar to stepping into a stream blindfolded. You know there are rocks in the stream that are there to support your crossing. Eventually your courage builds enough so you can take that first important step, that leap of faith. You must now rely solely on your faith in order to cross the stream. Amazingly, your foot finds a rock. Confidence starts to build. You feel safe in this moment, but what of the next? Can you move through your fear long enough to take the next step? Your journey to living your soul's purpose is comprised of many small steps. You take another step. Your foot feels something solid underneath, but you find you have to change your balance to step securely on the rock. This process gets repeated, continually testing your faith that all you need to support you is there, and your courage, which moves you toward your goal. It also assesses your willingness to allow for changes, to move to and fro just enough to come to a different point of balance.

Balancing with both feet planted firmly on the ground is easy. When you set out to claim your soul's purpose, you quickly find out that you need to relearn what it means to be balanced. You may ask yourself, "where is my center, where is my support?" Once you take the first big step, your former support system is gone. There is no support to grab onto, no family, friends, co-workers, or familiar structure to your life. Old attitudes and beliefs are erased. "Who am I?" is a question that gets asked from moment to moment. Who I am now is different than who I was a moment ago. Change becomes the familiar structure.

At times the path becomes narrow. Only those with sure-footed steps can traverse it. It takes courage and a clear mind. Dedication to the path yields many rewards. They are not easily seen, just as the path is not easy. Slowly, the path becomes wider and each step becomes easier.

If the wind is at your back, you can travel effortlessly many miles. When the wind blows in your face, it is hard to breathe and the path seems longer. The distance between you and your destination seems greater. Soon your mind doubts your heart. What was clear becomes muddy. Your faith is tested once more. To keep the wind at your back, you need to know the direction of the wind. Which way does the universe ask you to go? How do you know you have chosen the correct way? It is in the ease of each step, the steady unfolding of events and circumstances that you know could not be chance. It is the feeling of peace in the midst of chaos, the courage to come face to face with fear, and then, walk into it.

Slowly you begin to take deeper breaths, find your center in this moment with more ease, and then taking the next step becomes easier. You are so tuned into the process that before you know it, you have crossed the stream. You passed this test of faith. It will probably be your biggest test. The universe says, "Good job." Now your real work begins.

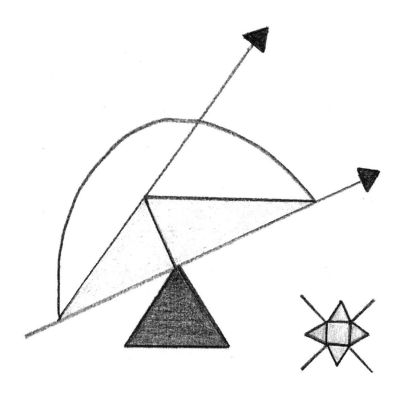

▲ PURPOSE ▲

Key 2

Climbing a mountain can
only be accomplished
with its permission.

▲ REFLECT ▲

The rain washes all things clean. It nourishes
the soul. Without it we cannot live or see our
reflection in a pond. Our bodies are cleansed,
our minds purged, our souls justified. One
drop is a mirror to the soul. Look carefully at a
drop of water on a flower. You will see the entire flower in that single drop. Similarly, look at
your reflection in a pool. Who do you see? Do
you know this person? Does the person reflect
who you think you are? The one is known by
the many. Who knows you? Do you allow yourself to be known, in all your perceived frailties
and shortcomings? Do you give yourself permission to be known as love and compassion,

as eternal and beautiful? Who gets to know the real you? How do you decide? Why do you filter things you don't want anyone to see? Perhaps they are in need of a mirror. Be that drop of water, that reflecting pool for each other. Dare to show your true self. Think of how much you will help others see their own truth. What if you allowed them to touch you? Would they feel your essence? Would they know that what they feel in you is in them as well? What about your words? Let the vibrations of your heart ring forth and allow other hearts to resonate with yours. You are beauty incarnate. You are majesty in form. You are the eternal silence in form and each has his or her own song, own frequency of vibration pulsing endlessly out into the universe. You are the composer, the conductor, the orchestra and the singer as well. You all carry your unique tune into the world. Together we all harmonize, with clear intent to do so. As we vibrate together, our frequencies begin to resonate until the ineffable is attained. In this moment, harmony is restored.

▲ REFLECT ▲

Key 3

A rose petal is nothing more
than the extraction of light
from its source.

▲ UNFOLD ▲

In spring, everything begins anew. The snows
of the winter of our forgetfulness are gone, leaving their life-giving water for the beauty to come.
Beauty is unfolding before your eyes. See it in
your heart and feel the beauty that resides there
and mingles with your own beauty. Look again.
Do you see yourself in that flower, that tree, that
blade of grass? Beauty is but one way to come
into oneness. Truth is another. Instead of looking, this requires listening. The truth can be
heard in your heart. It sings a song of joy, of
compassion, of resonance with what is. This is
truth: accepting what is, without judgment. It is
allowing the light to shine on everything so that

it can be seen in a new light. Isn't your definition of truth changing? It will continue to change as more and more light is cast on the earth. You are the bringers of this light and the makers of your truth. When all things become clear to you again, you come into oneness once more.

Oneness can also be felt in your heart through compassion. The act of sending love without judgment very quickly brings you to the oneness you had forgotten. The mere act of compassion dissolves separation. When you see a friend in her most desperate hour, you see yourself. When you meet someone on the street who is homeless, you see yourself. When you see a child lost in the joyous moment of now, giving his full attention to a tiny toy, you see yourself. You are all of these things and more.

Renew your own vision of who you think you are. Take the time to open your heart to yourself, look inside and see the divine spark that has been waiting to be fed.

▲ UNFOLD ▲

▲ ILLUMINATE ▲

A candle's flame is the pure combustion of air and matter. Its brightness depends upon the size of the wick and the amount of air present. The light you bring to the world is similar. It depends on your willingness to allow the consumption of matter in order to transmute it into light. Bring your attention to the space surrounding you. Is it free from obstructions? Does it allow for the free flow of air and energy?

You are all being asked to release lower frequency, denser thoughts. These are consumed by the light from many candles, not just your own. Release them with gratitude, knowing there are other flames assisting your own to transmute these frequencies. The denser, darker frequencies become the fuel for the flame, and as each of you assists one another in her or his release, more light is generated. The light consumes the dark and slower frequencies can no longer exist. This is your job. This is how you bring more light to the world. You are the eternal flame of truth, and with the light of this flame, the truth of who you are is illuminated.

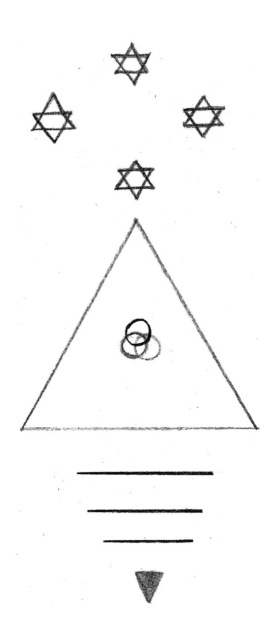

▲ ILLUMINATE ▲

Key 4

A bear cannot hibernate forever.

▲ HEARTMONIZE ▲

Today is the dawn of a new era. An unimagi-
nable journey into the depths of your soul is
transpiring here and now. The journey is that
of spiraling down into the core of the earth, the
core of your being, into creation's womb. See
her majesty and beauty. She is waiting for you,
each of you, to step into the womb of life, the
oneness that created you. You are held ever so
gently in the love of her belly. She knows you
are waiting too. Each one is called to enter in
her or his time. Each one removes the veil from
her or his eyes and walks into the oneness with
eyes wide open. A vision appears that was unseen to most. At this point in your awakening,

the heavenly ones sing a song of transcendence to open your hearts and your minds to what was always in front of you, what was always a part of you. What was forgotten is remembered. What was feared is now adored. All walls of separation crumble before your eyes. Everyone and everything you have ever known is there with you now. You may feel like a giant magnet, attracting every moment of your life, your entire life, what you call past, present, and future, to you now in this instant. Time no longer exists. Distance no longer exists. These you made up in your mind as a means of convincing yourself that you are separate. You forgot your oneness, your connection to everything, everywhere. You were walking around in a dream that you created to facilitate sleep. The moment of awakening has arrived! Wake up! Wake up! See the truth of who you are, see the beauty of who you are! There is nothing that is not you! Sip from your cup that overflows. Understand and feel how powerful you are. No matter what you conjure up in your mind, you are that. The most beautiful rose, the most inspiring sunrise, the child that loves everything without condition. It is all you. Now is the time to embrace all, everything that has, does, and ever will exist, the all of all. You are asked to accept that everything is you.

Open to the one source of all — the energy of love. At the heart of who you are is a love song that has always been resonating. As the frequency of the planet increases, you will hear your unique song become louder and louder. Sing out your song of love. Listen as others begin to sing theirs. The word "heart" is the word "hear" with a "t" on the end. Soon we will all "heartmonize" the planet. Mother Earth will hear us and respond with her love. We are creating a musical "peace." In order to complete the harmony, each person must sing his or her own unique song of love. Now the melody is complete and the piece (peace) is complete. Peace is as simple as singing your own unique song of love.

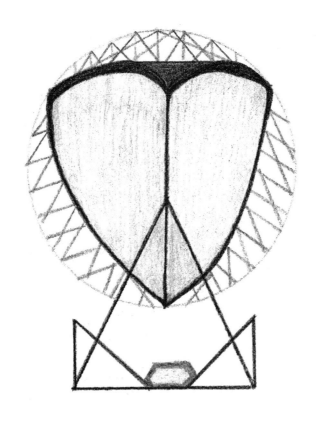

▲ HEARTMONIZE ▲

▲ FLOW ▲

You climb the mountain to see the sea and its beautiful raging waters. You come to the shore to see the waves come ever closer to you. The waves touch your feet, and the pull of the ocean moves like waves through your whole body. It coaxes you to come closer. You take a few more steps away from the shore toward the ocean. The pull is stronger. You begin to long to become one with the waves. You are at peace.

This is the flow that is happening now. There are waves of oneness gently coming over you now. You feel them as a burst of joy, a quiet moment of gratitude or a feeling of pure contentment with your life. Have you felt these recently? More are coming. The energies of the earth are changing, and the universal consciousness is calling you to come and play. The beauty, the majesty of the one consciousness is so strong, so enormous, that everyone will hear its call. As the waves of love wash over you, be open and grateful! The time of your transformation draws near! Soon the pull will be so great, you will forget your fear and move toward the resonance of your being. Come into harmony with that which you are, leave behind the muffled illusions of your reality, and open to that which is.

The waves are stronger now. They come more frequently. Allow them to permeate your being.

Feel the joy and the longing of your soul to return to whence it came. Do the animals question why they need to migrate thousands of miles or to swim upstream? To be in harmony is to go with the flow of the waves, to follow the patterns of life as they unfold. You are merely following your heart. Your heart created the patterns you follow. Choose peace and harmony, and the patterns form one way. Choose chaos and fear, and patterns develop differently. Your return to the oneness is assured, my loves. How you arrive is up to you. You can follow the waves of love, of light, of peace you have set in motion, or you may wallow in your illusion of fear. Your burdens are light if you follow the light. If you choose to remain in darkness, your journey will be slower and filled with uncertainty. Are you certain of your essence? Do you know who you really are? You are called to awaken to your true self, your essential nature, in concert with all that is. Listen to the calling of your heart. It beats in resonance with the divine oneness. You have never left the source of all. You merely forgot you are part of it. You are separate no more. You are the reason for the waves, for the longing, for the joy, for the opening. Walk into your awakening as though you just awoke from a short nap. Wipe away the mist of denial, the clouds of separation, and look upon your true self for the first time. Welcome all that is you with open arms, open heart, and open mind. Behold the beauty that is you.

▲ FLOW ▲

33

Key 5

The ground is a conveyor
of truth to all who listen.

▲ CREATOR ▲

(These words were inspired by a visit to Luray Caverns, Luray, Virginia.)

I entered the womb of Mother Earth and felt her hold my entire being in awe and ecstasy. I traveled deep within her and it felt like I returned home. Everything was familiar: her moist surface, her folded formations, and her resounding beauty. She told me a story as I walked through her caverns. "I am the mother of all. Here is where you will find your beauty, the truth of who you are. All that is within me is within you. All that shines from me shines from you. Your song is my song. It is the song of ages, the eternal word still ringing in the silence. Feel my love. Feel my power. They are yours as well."

In the depths of the earth I saw Atlantis rising. The dream of Atlantis, its illusion on the water projected from the stalactites above, never left. It lives within Mother Earth. She has cared for it all these years. The time for its return draws near. The time for a new continent, arising from the ocean fresh and new, is upon us.

Incredible bliss permeates all of my cells as I walk deeper into the womb. She continually sends her love, and I feel it take me to ecstasy. The entire journey feels like I am making love with her. She sings out in the most angelic and primal tones, and I am brought to tears with her. Her tear falls to my throat. I am purified once more. Once more I remember that I am she, and she is me. We are one now through this union, and as I make my way back through her caverns, I feel her wrap her arms around me. I am one with Mother Earth.

All the hopes, all the dreams of humanity rest actualized within her. It is by faith alone that the underground columns form. It is with this faith that I bring her forth in her healing and the healing of all that dwell upon her. My desire is for everyone to feel the respect I feel for her, and to feel the love that reminds me I am not separate from her or those that dwell upon her.

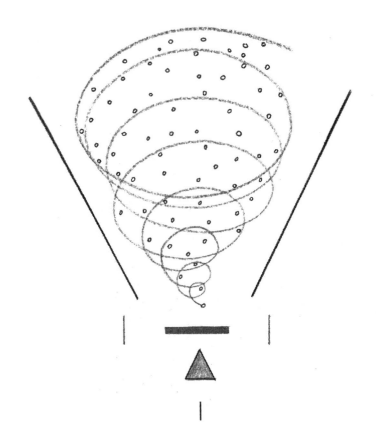

▲ CREATOR ▲

▲ CHANGE ▲

The earth is changing now. Love her in her transition. Love the rain, love the tremors, love the volcanoes, love the wind, and love the storms. She is cleansing. She is readying herself for her rebirth, renewal and new life. Do as Mother Earth does; shed all the things that hold you back from your true self. It is time to let go. Mother Earth is ready for all of you to release the bonds of forgetfulness. She is in a place of change, and all of the forgetfulness will be transmuted into remembering. After all, isn't that what you and Mother Earth are doing now, re-membering? She is putting the pieces of a forgotten past into the present. She is taking her hand and wiping away every tear. She is holding each of you in her loving arms. Return to her and feel her love, not her wrath. Feel her compassion for life and not her destruction. Transmute the pain into joy. The time for your transformation is now.

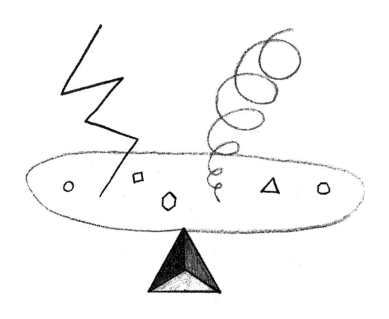

▲ CHANGE ▲

▲ LISTEN ▲

Because you came here at this time, you are heroes, all of you. Because you chose this path on the road to enlightenment, be glad. The time approaches. You are given all of the tools to be in concert with the vibrations of change. Look to the sky daily. It will tell you what to wear and what to bring with you for the day. Listen to the birds. Their song tells you what approaches — whether to be cautious or light hearted. Feel the earth beneath your feet. Let it rise to your center. Do you feel uneasy, dizzy, calm, or safe? What will come to you today? Use your most gifted sense to know how to proceed each day. Bring the forces of nature together within you and through you. Become one with your world. Trust your intuition.

Give yourself permission to align your body with your mind. Do not allow your mind to overrule your body. The body holds the ancient wisdom of life. Honor it. Let your mind wait for the body to tune into the surrounding vibrations. Then let the mind interpret. Not analyze, interpret. It is only a means to construct the energies in a matrix that is understandable to you. Once you have done this, act upon it. This solidifies the pattern in your body. Allow only truth to be absorbed in the body. Truth resonates at a higher frequency than most other sensations. This is how you know it is truth. Does it ring true for you? Does it resonate with you? Listen to your words. They are more literal than you think. Once truth has reverberated within your body, it sets up a pattern of sacred geometry that is conveyed to the DNA.

Love is the only energy that resonates higher than truth. Love's power washes over all and removes any impurities or blockages to hearing and living one's truth. To pay attention to your truth is to send love to yourself. Receiving love from you is easy. But first you must be open to acknowledging your divinity. Can you allow your mind to entertain such a thought? If the mind, body and spirit are not in alignment with the concept of self-love, then you cannot experience it. Only through experience can you truly embody the essence of the energy. Once this is done, it will resonate with the rest of you, your mind and spirit as well. Your mind is the gatekeeper. What you allow in or out is subject to be scrutinized by your mind. To open the gate, you must first relax your body. Then call in your higher self for guidance. This energy will engage your higher frequencies and make connection and assimilation easier. Congruency comes when two frequencies emerge as one through the meeting at similar wavelengths. When two waves converge with the same frequency from opposite directions they cancel each other out. If they merge from the same direction they amplify. Only serve to amplify the frequency.

Do you listen to your words? Do they speak their truth to you? Who else can speak your truth but you? Can anyone know what is in your heart? Your heart knows what no one else has seen. Trust your inner knowing, your feelings of truth.

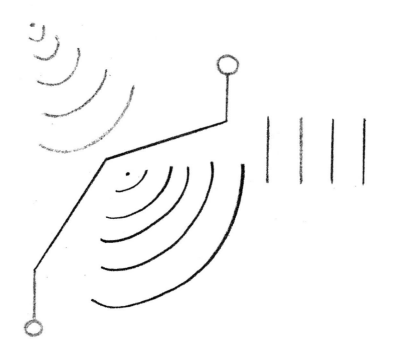

▲ LISTEN ▲

Key 6

When all is quiet, all that can
be heard is the rising of the sun.

▲ CALLING ▲

It grows brighter each day, your love for life
and for yourself, so bright that the light must
shine forth from you. You are now the light of
life. Let your spirit soar to the infinite. Release
all bonds, boundaries, borders, and beliefs.
Renounce all that places restrictions on your
limitlessness. See your unlimited glory as a
vast array of causal energies coming to your
aid each time you think. The cosmos is not
bounded. You are not bounded, for the cosmos
is in you. Release all your fears of greatness. It
is your former self that cries out in the night,
"I can't, I can't!" Who you are will not let that
voice be heard any longer.

The stillness holds all motion. The silence holds all sound. Be still and know your God Self. Listen to your heart. Let it be heard. It sings the song of everlasting joy, peace and love. Listen to the silence. All messages come from the nowhere, the nothingness, the void. You pick the one that calls to you, for only you can hear it. It is your "calling." Why do you think this word is used for your divine purpose? The silence calls you forth with its divine message for you alone. Listen to the voice of God that runs through your veins. Only you know the melody. Only you can sing the song. Once you sing, others around you begin to search for their song. Once everyone sings their own song, answers their unique calling, the world will resonate in harmony. The choir is complete and the peace orchestrated.

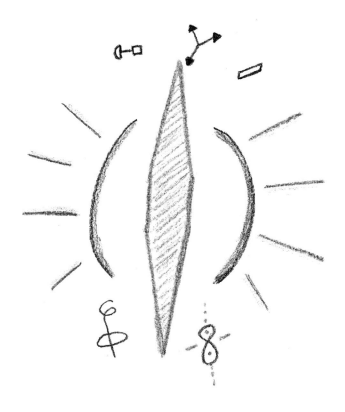

▲ CALLING ▲

Key 7

Joy resides in the heart.

▲ JOY ▲

The new day has started. No longer shall you live in fear of what appears to be real, for you know what is real. The truth of who you are is but a breath away. Feel your lungs expand with the fresh clean air of a new day. Feel it permeate every cell of your being. The breath cleanses you. Allow it to move out any stagnant energy and start sweeping out the cobwebs in your mind. It is time to wake up your mind and let it breathe. Let it expand infinitely in all directions. Why have you limited yourself for so long? Feel and sense who you really are. There are no limits. There are no boundaries in the universe. You, my dear ones, placed them on yourselves. Pull apart the seeming mess of chains and untangle the life force, the omniscient self that is waiting patiently for its freedom. Free your mind from bondage and allow the breath of a new day to enter into your body for the first time. Expand your lungs. Expand your heart. Expand your mind. Only your thought about yourself holds you back. Not anyone else's thought about you, but your own thought about yourself. If you created it, you have power over it to change it! Think a new thought that is all encompassing, all loving, all powerful, and all knowing. You are not separate from God. Stop the illusion. You are part of the One that created you. If God is all knowing, all loving, all powerful, all en-compassing, then so are you. You are made in the image and likeness of God. Believe in who you are!

Step into the dawn of a new day. Let its light shine upon you and en-lighten you. It is time to wake up from your illusion of powerlessness, of limits, of unworthiness. Who are you but who you think you are? Accept that you are a co-creator with God. Know that the universe waits upon your command. Allow the glory that is you to shine forth. Come into the light of love. See yourself for the first time and marvel at your beauty. Make the world smile.

Joy comes from living the truth of who you are. Joy is contagious. Be the bearer of good news to your community. Spread the joy of who you are. This is how you can be the beacon of light. Become one with your joy and feel the connecting power of joy spread out in all directions. Notice the web of joy you have created and how easily you created it. Living in joy is living in the light. Remove your worn out suit of armor that shielded you from yourself and don your coat of joy. This coat does not separate like the armor but says, "Come and play!" Joy needs to be shared! The wind is able to carry your joy because it is light! The wind cannot carry the armor of separation. Allow the false façade to melt away. Remove the filters of illusion. Return to the child inside that cries to be set free. Children have no armor and no filters. Their innocent perception is their joy. Joy-n with them. Joy is a way back to oneness, to the connectedness of all. Smile!

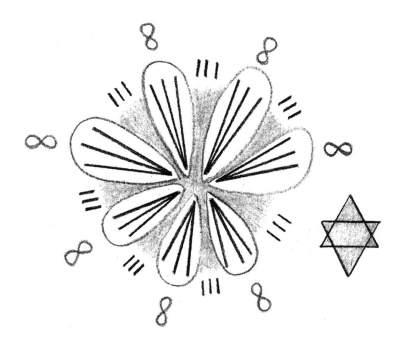

▲ JOY ▲

▲ ENVISION ▲

What is the color of joy? How do you name it? It comes gently on a breeze and creates a large wind in your being. Once there, it remains as long as you give life to it. What is the color of life? Is it fire-colored, bright orange-red or is it green like the tree? Paint your own life and joy will find its own resident resonance. Paint your life with bold, bright colors, wide and long. Let the brush flow, as it will. Notice the shapes you make. Notice the colors you choose.

This is how you see your life now. You envision it. You bring it into sight by placing it on paper. The painting of your life is your joy. You obtain joy by looking at it in amazement. Am I that beautiful, you say? Yes, and more! Your painting is part of a collage of paintings from each person. It is like painting an individual puzzle piece without knowing what the finished puzzle looks like. Once all of the paintings of everyone everywhere come together, the puzzle is complete and the image is shown.

What the image looks like is dependent on what each person paints. If a lot of dark colors are used in individual paintings, the final image is dark and shadowy. If a lot of bright colors are used, the final image is light and joyous, envisioning for us all the light and joy of peace. Do you see now how your joy adds to the joy and peace of all? Once all of the pieces are arranged, notice what you all have created. Do you see how easy it is to create peace? After all, peace can also be spelled p i e c e. It takes each one of you to work in harmony. Here is your peace. Now go and make it happen!

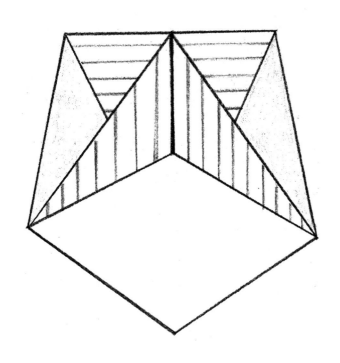

▲ ENVISION ▲

Key 8

Cast your net upon
the sea and let your
faith feed you.

▲ SIGHT ▲

The blessings of those chosen to bring forth the light are here. They fall upon those who hear the words of truth. Riches pour forth now. All are bathed in the light of compassion. It is happening before your eyes. Each day it is written anew. Your wake-up call is here now. What message is sent to you today? How will you know it is time? Be patient and wait for your own opening to show you the way of truth. Walk it, this path you are shown. It is the walk of compassion, the journey of love. This is why you came — to be the love of God on earth. Whenever someone looks into your eyes, they will see the light of love. Whenever someone hears your words, they play the strings of the heart and sing love. Whenever you touch someone, they feel the joy of compassion, the freedom of forgiveness, the flow of life, the energy of love that moves through you and is you. Bestow on the many what the few have, until now, experienced. Allow the light of love to settle into your bones and set up permanent residence and resonance within you. Bring it forth from the depths of who you are so that others may know who they are. Only in this mirroring can others see their own divinity.

You are God's mirror. Your job is to keep it clean so that a perfect image may be reflected. The cleansing is done by anchoring yourself in your vision and allowing that vision to be the physical you. In this way, each day is new, each day another aspect of your beauty shines forth. This is the blessing that you bestow on the many. What else is awakening but the opening of one's eyes and heart to what is. The truth has been hidden. Now it is time for it to shine forth.

▲ SIGHT ▲

▲ CONCEPT ▲

Can you imagine a world so enormous, so vast, that you cannot enumerate it? Can you imagine a world so new and so beautiful that there are no words to describe it? Open your mind to infinite possibilities, to unbounded love, to everlasting peace. Come to a place where time and space have no meaning, where thought is the mover, where everything is transformed into the truth of what is. Embrace it all with open arms and open minds.

What you will see cannot be comprehended by your present mindset. You must let go of all preconceptions, all old patterns and habits. We are transitioning from the conceived thought to the unconceived. Until now, your mind could only function in a matrix of preconceptions. These must be removed to allow what has not yet been conceived to enter your mind, to bring it into "concept-ion" and give it life.

Why do you sit in despair when the world is calling to you to open your eyes to a new world, a new way? What was is past. Come into the now. Let go of all that held you in darkness, all that limited your perception of yourself. Free yourself from your own doing, your own chains, and your own bondage. Love is the key. Truth is the answer. Choose to change and rejoice in the change. Only through the complete acceptance of what is can you pass through the gates of the new kingdom. What you will see has always been there. What has changed is your thinking, and this higher level of consciousness removes the veils to a vaster and more beautiful universe.

▲ CONCEPT ▲

▲ CO-CREATION ▲

How can a willow bend? Why does a frog leap? Why does truth follow beauty? How can a thought move mountains? Can a molecule of water exist as a vapor, liquid, and solid at the same time? Is everything consciousness? Does everything have a soul? Who or what orchestrates the cosmos? Does each person choose the hour of his or her awakening? Why are we here now?

The answers lie within each of us, waiting to be unearthed. As the first answer comes to the surface, it breaks the surface tension of the bubble of uncertainty and allows all other answers to float to the surface instantaneously. In one brief second, the answers to questions that have been asked for centuries are answered. Everyone is capable of finding the answers within. There is no need for study, higher degrees or higher IQ. Information flows so freely now that it is accessible to all by merely asking for it.

Thought is the vehicle through which manifestation occurs. Creation is a sea of endless potentialities, swimming around until thought comes and catches one. What is possible is determined by thought. Our minds can limit our potential or set us free. If we truly believe we can create our reality, then synchronicity happens immediately. The perceived time lapse between the thought and its manifestation is decreasing now. This time lapse facilitated your slumber and allowed for the illusion of powerlessness to pervade your minds until now. This is what it means to awaken.

You are the creator of your life story. Conscious co-creation is the enlightened state. The consequences of your thoughts become immediate. Haven't you been told, "ask and you shall receive?" Be careful what you ask for, because you <u>will</u> get it. The power you hold within your mind is proportional to your ability to open your mind. Break the false limits that family, friends, co-workers, society, government and religion placed before you.

Remember playing the game "what if" as a child? It seemed like a game then because you didn't see an immediate outcome to the thoughts. Even if you didn't play it as a child, how many of you have asked, "What if I won a million dollars?" You play this game often. Some of you choose to play the victim. The powerless version of the game is "if only." What if you could create anything you choose just by thinking of it? Well you can, and you have been doing this unconsciously your whole life. Now, you get to play the game consciously, realizing that everything you create will affect everything. Everything is connected; we are one. This is the guiding principle. Whatever you do for another, you do for yourself. You see, this is the ultimate win-win game. Since the consequences of your thoughts will become immediate, you will learn quickly that selfishness, greed, hate, revenge and the like are not in your best interest. There will be a short learning curve, and then peace will reign once again.

You will awaken to one of the most basic and powerful laws of the universe: we are all one. The great governor of our "newly found" power is love. You see, with love, all things are truly possible. Being in love is your connection to Source. Love embraces all life and intends for life its highest good, trusting that each creation has the innate wisdom to know what is in its own best interest. It is in the allowing, the surrender to your divine plan, that peace permeates each of our souls. We now enter the cosmic mind of unity consciousness and assume the role of conscious co-creator.

▲ CO-CREATION ▲

▲ INDIVIDUATED ▲

As your body vibrates at higher frequencies, it is natural to feel a loss and a void in your life. You are releasing the old to allow the new to come in. The loss you may feel comes from knowing and accepting that what was is gone, and who you were in relation to that is no longer. The void you think you created is an illusion, for what could you be void of? The entire universe rests within you, and you in the universe. What could you want? It just feels like a void to your present human consciousness. This is the way the human body processes this frequency of information. It is a new frequency to the body, and it cannot process it using the constructs of the past. Therefore it leaves the body with a longing, a question, a perceived void. It is the body's way of saying, "I'm not done processing that information, please stand by." It is experiencing temporary technical difficulty until the codes necessary for its completion come in. These codes come into existence through your expanded consciousness. You call them forth. This is, in essence, what self-love is, a calling forth of your true essence, to be more of who you are.

You are the individuated genius of an energy matrix from the vast Source of all. No one has the exact same manifestation of codes as you. You have your own unique resonant blueprint in the cosmos. There is no other source to draw upon but the one that is you, in you, and created your unique blueprint. The universe of endless possibilities would feel a void if your uniqueness ceased to exist. This, my dear friends, is not possible. You are part of the eternal consciousness that is the "I am that I am."

Dare to rise above your limited eyes and see through the eyes of one who remembers. See the infinite possibilities that await your decision to manifest them into your reality. Make friends with your infinite self. The small self who succumbed to scarcity consciousness and fear is being transformed into the higher self of truth and expanded awareness of the infinite. You are your only limitation. You are the author of your life. The people you meet, the experiences you have, the prosperity you allow — all are determined by you. You choose the characters you meet, circumstances and experiences. Rewrite your life to allow your story to unfold in such a way as to remember your own glory, live your truth, and abide in your love and light that is the spine of your autobiographical book.

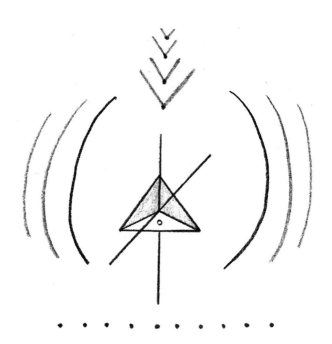

▲ INDIVIDUATED ▲

Key 9

When a plum reaches ripeness,
it cannot hide its sweetness.

▲ PERFECTION ▲

Perfection is not based on an instantaneous moment, a single snapshot in time. It is an ongoing thread that is woven in the fabric of time. You must stand back and see the bigger picture to envision perfection. Do not judge the moment, for you are not capable now of seeing the greater picture, the holographic web of life that connects everything to the one. Just as dropping a pebble affects the lake, every action you take affects the whole of creation. You cause ripples to flow out from you. The person next to you does the same, and so on. The holographic pattern produced by this unending series of events cannot be perceived with your current mind. Open to the possibility that the combination of events is infinite, and any and all patterns are possible. It is in the conscious choosing of actions or effects that changes the pattern. As we all come into unity conscious-ness, the patterns of peace, harmony and love will be imbedded in the web of life. The thoughts are the cause; the pattern of peace is the effect. This is how you create a thousand years of peace. Do you now see the perfection? Could it be seen in the opening and closing of a camera shutter, taking a snapshot of a child witnessing the death of his parents, in the rag-ing seas, or in the crumbling mountains? The pattern has not yet completed in the matrix. Allow it to come to completion, and all will see the perfection in every instant, in every event or circumstance. Now you have come to con-sensus or come to your senses. You all agreed on the pattern, on the image, on the outcome. This is unity consciousness: seeing the pattern in the everyday, minute-to-minute unfolding of life. The agreement is signed by all. There is nothing else to see but what all of you create. This is perfection. The circle is now complete. All is truly one.

▲ PERFECTION ▲

▲ CONNECTION ▲

What is at the depths of your soul? Can you feel a long cylinder where your longing resides? It follows your spine and slowly makes its way up, vertebrae by vertebrae. There is a force at your core that pulses and sends waves slowly up your spine. The force is love, a pure acceptance of your longing. It makes no judgment; it places no constraints or conditions on it. It accepts your longing as it is and where it is. The force of love is not one of pushing or moving forward, but one of opening and allowing. As more love fills your core, your longing is allowed to move up toward the surface. Up into your gut so you can sense it, feel it, empower it. Up to your heart where you can become one with it and open yourself to yourself. At the throat, you can give voice to it, using your will to give it a name. At your third eye, the vision of your longing becomes clear. The reasons are now evident. Once it reaches your crown, the journey continues to the higher energies that connect you to the Source of All. The longing is now merged with the oneness that called it forth, and is transformed into the remembrance of who you are and the acceptance of your divinity.

By accepting who you really are, you also accept the assignment you chose before your forgetting. It is the reason you embodied. It is your soul purpose to be that which you chose, to complete your part of the whole, to play the role you agreed to play. It is the completion of the circles within your life. Once the longing is moved through all of your chakras, they now vibrate higher, in full remembrance of their original, essential frequency. Each cell follows their call, their beat. Soon your entire body radiates light. You are filled with passion for your purpose, and your passion is the bliss that you feel. You have once more connected to the matrix of the one consciousness, to the Source of All. Now all things flow easily to you, as you desire them. You are in the flow. You found your exact coordinates on the grid and connected your pathway to the divine. The process leads you back to yourself, to the connection of all, to the oneness that is you.

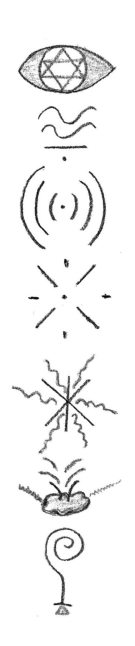

▲ CONNECTION ▲

▲ ONENESS ▲

From the smallest seed, a giant tree is born. From the darkest night, the brightest light is seen. Shed the veils of illusion; see who you are. You are the acorn and the tree, the dark and the light. There is no more duality. There is no more this or that. There is just the all, the everything that is you. The time for separation is passed. Come into the light of oneness. Remember your part of the whole, of the interconnectedness of life. You cannot exist without the sun, without water, without the earth, without all that surrounds you, because it is you. The ocean can be seen in a single drop of water with the eyes of oneness. The desert is entirely held within a tiny grain of sand. Without the sand, the desert could not exist and without the desert, the sand would have no meaning. The all and the one must exist simultaneously. Your connection with the source of the oneness gives meaning to your life. It is in the connecting, the remembering, that we become whole, part of the all, and in the process, healed.

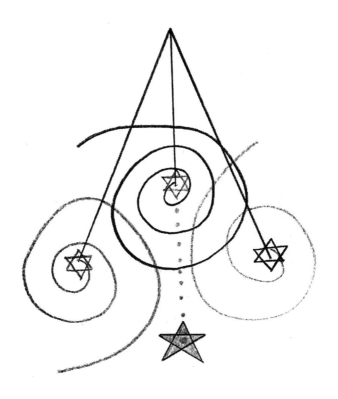

▲ ONENESS ▲

Afterthoughts

I noticed a bald eagle circling overhead as I was driving to one of my favorite hiking places, two years after I had written the keys. I parked my car, walked to the edge of the railing, and located the eagle circling in the distance. As I asked him to fly toward me, he immediately flew directly to me, circled, and then flew off. It was clear this was an auspicious moment and I was to pay attention.

The eagle is one of my totems. The Romans associated the eagle with Jupiter, the planet of expanded good fortune of all kinds. The eagle in Egyptian hieroglyphics symbolized the soul or spirit. In early Christian mysticism, it was the symbol of resurrection. To the Hopis, it is the greatest of all birds. Seeing an eagle means one's life will take a powerful new direction and will experience a heightened responsibility for one's spiritual growth.

As I walked along the trail, I pondered what this particular sighting meant to me. I thought, "The eagle does not doubt his ability to fly to new heights. He doesn't even think about it all. Flying is part of him. It is part of his essence, and an eagle does not question who he is."

When you know who you truly are, unfold your layers to your core, and live your true essence, there is no need to ask the question, "Who am I?" You are living in the key of life.

In Gratitude

I am supported and blessed by so many wonderful beings that it is difficult to name them all. One person has absolutely been a catalyst for my writings. Within a month of arriving in Sedona, I received two sessions from Mark David Gerson. He is a master at translating the language of light into sacred geometry drawings, using his voice to bring forth the vibrational tones that the drawings represent. He is also a master of the word, having authored the mystical fantasy, *The MoonQuest*. Several people had suggested I make an appointment to see him. After receiving a language of light activation and a writing activation session, I allowed the words inside of me to flow. It is time for these words to be read, to be heard, to be felt. Mark David, my soul sings songs of joy and gratitude for you.

My friend, Jason Boles, a gifted sound healer and graphic artist, created the awesome and powerful cover of this book. His creations are the ultimate in alchemical magic! Many, many blessings to you, Jason!

Many thanks to my interior book designer, Rudy Ramos, whose patience and proficiency is second to none!

My fellow lightworkers, goddesses and friends, Cindy and Karen, are my earth angels, and lovingly guided and supported me during the writing of this book. A special thank you to Karen for your editing skills. What better editor could I ask for but a double Virgo! Cindy and Karen, you are part of my lifeblood, the holy grail of communion with the divine. Blessings to you, and I love you.

My eternal gratitude goes to God, the Prime Creator, Source of All. Thank you for always taking impeccable care of me, especially when my human fears made it difficult for me to trust in you and myself. Acknowledging the use of my power as a co-creator, and surrendering into the flow of my creation, has made all the difference in my life. Now we are co-creators of beauty.

About the Author

Joan Cerio is a mystic, healer and way-shower, who devotes her life to helping others. She holds a graduate degree in science education and an undergraduate degree in biology, which provide the conceptual and energetic balance between the physical and spiritual in her life.

Having worked in the health and healing professions for over 30 years, Joan has served as an intuitive holistic practitioner in the capacity of Reiki Master Teacher, Integrated Energy Therapy Practitioner and Licensed Massage Therapist for wellness centers, chiropractors, and in private practice.

Joan has expanded her understanding of the wisdom of the ages through numerous bodywork and spiritual classes, among which are "Flower of Life." Along with her own intuitive gifts, she incorporated methods and concepts learned from them, and integrated them into her knowledge of sacred geometry and sound to create a unique healing experience. She has taught secondary science and massage therapy and continues to teach Reiki and numerous metaphysical workshops.

Joan is developing a school of self-mastery based upon the keys you have just read. If you are interested in discovering more about your core essence, the truth of who you are, or if you would like more information about Joan, upcoming *In the Key of Life* events, her blog, Key of Life elixir, or new books, please go to:

www.joancerio.com

Joan resides in Sedona, Arizona.

Appendix

Additional Activation Tool
Key of Life
Vibrational Support Elixir

This vibrational support elixir was co-created with Anna Rita Raineri, founder of Sedona Sacred Arts. Taking the Key of Life elixir assists in maintaining the higher frequency of energy that has been activated in you by reading this book. The elixir can be taken like a flower essence, 1-3 drops under the tongue, placed directly on the skin, in drinking water, or added to massage oil or lotion.

If you are interested in purchasing the elixir, please go to:

www.joancerio.com

How it was created

With the intention of reminding the users of their divinity, a vessel of purified water was placed within a 3-dimensional six-foot copper star tetrahedron or merkaba (hexagram) and imprinted with energy. More energy was then imprinted by toning the Middle Pillar Activation from the Qabalah. Your divine essence is connected to your DNA, the blueprint of life. The use of this elixir activates your DNA to allow you to vibrate at the higher frequencies that are coming in now.

Most of the building blocks of organic chemistry (the chemistry of living things) form benzene rings that are in the shape of hexagons. If the lines of a hexagon are extended they form a hexagram or star tetrahedron.

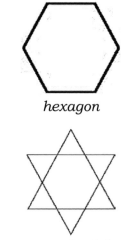

hexagon

hexagram or star tetrahedron

DNA is made of atoms whose bonding configurations form hexagons (the base part of the structure).

The 4 amino acid bases of DNA

This is how the star tetrahedron and DNA are related. The energy around your body forms the geometric shape of a star tetrahedron or merkaba. It is through this sacred geometry that you connect to the universe. The merkaba is your light spirit body, and its geometry holds the energy of ascension, allowing you to travel to different dimensions.

The Middle Pillar Activation from the Qabalah activates the charkas, or major energy centers of the body. The middle pillar refers to the middle vertical line in the Tree of Life and to the middle vertical line in our bodies where the prana tube is located.

Toning the Hebrew words to this activation opens the chakras. The Hebrew words remind us of our divinity.

Qabalah

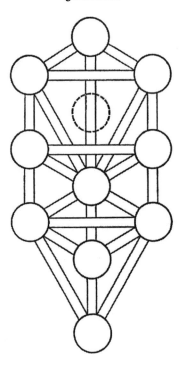

The 'Tree of Life'